Learning space with 3d GEOSHAPES™

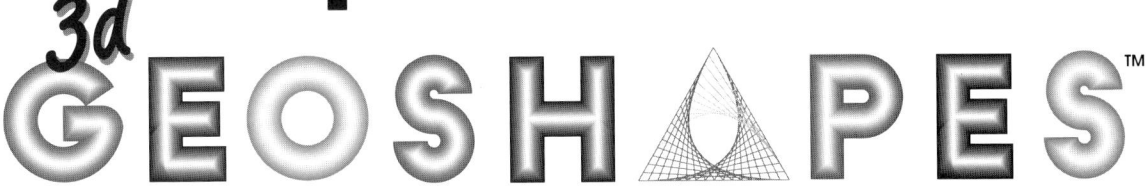

UPPER PRIMARY 3-6

ILLUSTRATOR   BARBARA JENKINS
EDITOR   DOUG WILLIAMS

Limited Reproduction Permission:

Permission to duplicate this material is limited to the person who purchases this book or for whom this book was purchased.

© 1995 3D GEOSHAPES AUSTRALIA PTY LTD

First published 1995

Produced by: Pam Madner

Published by:

3D GEOSHAPES AUSTRALIA
25 FIRST AVENUE
SUNSHINE
VICTORIA 3020

Printed in Australia

ISBN 0 646 20588 9

Other publications:
Learning Space with 3D Geoshapes
Lower Primary P-2

3D Geoshapes ™ is the trademark of 3D Geoshapes Australia Pty. Ltd.
Worldwide patents and registered designs are pending or granted.

Introduction

The activities in this book were designed to develop children's concepts of spatial awareness, measurement and number skills, whilst also promoting cooperative group learning and problem-solving skills. 3D Geoshapes is an innovative educational construction system, currently consisting of triangles, squares, pentagons, hexagons and triangles used to build a two frequency geodesic dome. Its open skeleton design allows for easy construction and examination of networks. Teachers recognise 3D Geoshapes as a manipulative that could generate a wealth of positive learning experiences, "if only I had time to plan more rather than just build with them." It is the intention of this book to support teachers in exploring the richness promised by the material and therefore, hopefully, to play a part both in enriching children's learning and reducing the burden on teachers.

All activities have been suggested by teachers and tried out in classrooms. We know these activities work and we have attempted to assist you to see their connection with the overall curriculum by placing each task in the perspective of the National Statement on Mathematics.

All the activities use a similar format. The Teachers' Notes begin by outlining the strand and objectives, duration of activity, group size and materials required. The Teachers' Notes also include discussion notes related to implementing and assessing these activities. Follow-up ideas provide extensions and challenges. The Student Activity Sheets follow, and are complemented by a later section of ideas using 3D Geoshapes in a number of cross-curricula themes - the beach, our community, space, transport and dinosaurs.

The Student Activity Sheets have been written as simply as possible to encourage the children to govern their own learning. However, we envisage a partnership where we have found "the time to do more than just build with them", but we rely on you to positively intervene in the students' learning. The Teachers' Notes provide a basis for such intervention.

Acknowledgments
The publisher would like to thank Rob Vingerhoets and Michael Ymer for their contributions in developing and trialing the activities presented in this book.

The activities Tetrahedron Nets, Cube Nets, How Many Triangles?, Pointy Fences and Tetrahedron Triangles are used with permission of Curriculum Corporation. These materials are part of the Mathematics Task Centre Project. For further information about this project please call (03) 9 639 0699.

NATIONAL STATEMENT process strands	Can You Make It?	Tunnel Vision	Useful Machines	The Three Bears	Dream Home	Weak or Strong?	Fill in the Shape	Tile the Table	Finding Volumes	Stack 'em & Pack 'em	Four Room Apartments	View It Carefully	Tetrahedron Nets	Cube Nets	Nets, Pyramids & Prisms	Shape Sketch	From the Photo	What Value?	Count the Squares	Make It Bigger	How Many Triangles?	Pointy Fences	Tetrahedron Triangles
Attitudes & Appreciations																							
1 ... show a positive response to the use of mathematics as a tool in practical situations		■		■	■																		
2 ... demonstrate the confidence to apply mathematics and to gain knowledge about mathematics					■													■					
3 ... display a willingness and ability to work cooperatively with others and to value the contribution of others		■																					
4 ... exhibit a willingness to persist when solving problems and to try different methods of attack								■											■				
5 ... show an awareness that creativity and initiative are encouraged and valued within mathematics education					■																		
7 ... understand that mathematics involves observing, generalising and representing patterns																			■		■		■
8 ... appreciate that the economy and power of mathematical notation and terminology help in developing mathematical ideas	■																						
Mathematical Inquiry																							
B1 ... draw diagrams and read and write mathematics using simple formulae, pictures, tables and statistical graphs																						■	
B2 ... clarify, use and interpret mathematical expressions and phrases	■																						
B3 ... observe, represent and extend spatial and number patterns		■							■										■	■	■	■	■
B4 ... test conjectures in space and number and search for counter-examples							■		■	■	■						■						
B5 ... explain conjectures and results, using appropriate mathematical language		■																					
B8 ... undertake structured investigations, individually and collaboratively											■												
B9 ... use personal and group organisational skills to help in tackling mathematical problems			■	■																			
Choosing & Using Mathematics																							
B1 ... choose and use mathematical skills to make decisions														■	■			■	■			■	
B2 ... clarify and pose problems arising in practical or imagined contexts					■	■												■		■			
B4 ... verify and interpret solutions with respect to the original problem														■				■	■				

NATIONAL STATEMENT content strands	Can You Make It?	Tunnel Vision	Useful Machines	The Three Bears	Dream Home	Weak or Strong?	Fill in the Shape	Tile the Table	Finding Volumes	Stack 'em & Pack 'em	Four Room Apartments	View It Carefully	Tetrahedron Nets	Cube Nets	Nets, Pyramids & Prisms	Shape Sketch	From the Photo	What Value?	Count the Squares	Make It Bigger	How Many Triangles?	Pointy Fences	Tetrahedron Triangles
Space																							
B1 ... build structures and make geometric models, analysing their cross-sections and nets		■	■	■	■				■	■	■		■	■	■	■	■					■	■
B2 ... compare and classify objects, analyse their shapes and describe in conventional geometric language	■			■	■	■				■													
B4 ... compare and classify figures, analyse their shapes and describe in conventional geometric language							■													■			
B5 ... carry out rotations, translations and reflections and recognise and produce related symmetries							■	■				■											
B6 ... recognise congruent figures by superimposition, and informally investigate congruent figures								■	■														
B7 ... rearrange, fit together and tessellate figures and stack and pack objects								■	■	■	■												
B8 ... reduce and enlarge figures and objects and investigate distortions resulting from transformations																				■			
B9 ... produce, interpret and compare scale drawings and maps, and scale models of familiar structures		■																					
B10 ... interpret and produce two-dimensional representations of objects									■			■	■	■	■	■	■						
B12 ... plan and execute arrangements according to specifications	■																						■
Number																							
B1 ... use whole numbers and decimal fractions to count and order collections and measures																		■		■			
B2 ... recognise, produce and use patterns in number			■																	■			■
B8 ... remember basic addition and multiplication facts and perform mental computations on whole numbers and money																		■					
Measurement																							
B1 ... measure compare and order objects and events using length, capacity, mass, area, volume, time and angle		■	■			■			■														
B2 ... choose appropriate units for tasks by considering purpose, and the need for precision and/or communication				■					■											■			
Algebra																							
AB1 ... use verbal expressions (oral or written) to describe and summarise spatial or numerical patterns																			■		■		
AB2 ... make and use arithmetic generalisations		■																					
AB3 ... represent (verbally, graphically, in writing and physically) and interpret relationships between quantities																		■					

Contents

Can You Make It?	1
Tunnel Vision	4
Useful Machines	7
The Three Bears	9
Dream Home	11
Weak or Strong?	14
Fill in the Shape	18
Tile the Table	20
Finding Volumes	23
Stack 'em & Pack 'em	27
Four Room Apartments	31
View It Carefully	33
Tetrahedron Nets	35
Cube Nets	37
Nets, Pyramids & Prisms	39
Shape Sketch	42
From the Photo	46
What Value?	49
Count the Squares	51
Make It Bigger	54
How Many Triangles?	58
Pointy Fences	60
Tetrahedron Triangles	62
Theme Ideas: The Beach	64
Dinosaurs	65
Our Community	66
Space	68
Transport	70

Can You Make It?

TEACHERS' NOTES

Strand and Objectives

Attitudes
- appreciate that the economy and power of mathematical notation and terminology help in developing mathematical ideas

Space
- compare and classify objects, analyse their shapes and describe in conventional geometric language
- produce, interpret and compare scale drawings and maps, and scale models of familiar structures
- plan and execute arrangements according to specifications

Mathematical Inquiry
- clarify, use and interpret mathematical expressions and phrases

Duration   40 minutes

Group size   Pairs

Materials

8 triangles (4 colours x 2), 12 squares (6 colours x 2), an assortment of other Geoshapes and a screen such as a book per pair.

1. If children are unfamiliar with Geoshapes, allow free play first and then ask them to make cubes and tetrahedrons.
2. The purpose of these activities is to develop and refine mathematical language in a context. This language may vary depending on whether the partners are beside or opposite each other, so the children are asked to experience both situations. Encourage children to share their thoughts. eg: *Why was it difficult to give instructions? How did you feel when you saw that your model was exactly the same as your partner's?*

Follow-up Ideas

1. Combine the task with work on a communication theme and ask the children to give their instructions via a tin can telephone or in writing as if the Copier were in a distant place.
2. Repeat the activity making a 2D shape. In this case, combine Geoshapes with other materials, eg: pop sticks, blocks, buttons. The replica has to have these items in the same place as in the Maker's shape.
3. Repeat the activity using 12 pentagons each to complete a dodecahedron.

© 3D GEOSHAPES 1995

Can You Make It? A

* For this activity you will each need 6 squares - one of each colour. *

1. Sit *beside* your partner and use a book to hide what you are making. One person is the Maker and one person is the Copier.
2. The Maker builds a cube and gives instructions to the Copier to make a replica.
   A replica is exactly the same structure with the same colours in the same places.
3. Compare what you have made. What were the problems that caused any differences.
4. Swap jobs and try again.
5. Sit *opposite* each other and repeat the activity.
6. Do you have to use different language to be able to make a replica?

Can You Make It? B

* For this activity you will each need 4 triangles - one of each colour.*

1. Sit *beside* your partner and use a book to hide what you are making. One person is the Maker and one person is the Copier.
2. The Maker builds a tetrahedron like this: and gives instructions to the Copier to make a replica. *A replica is exactly the same structure with the same colours in the same places.*
3. Compare what you have made. What were the problems that caused any differences.
4. Swap jobs and try again.
5. Sit *opposite* each other and repeat the activity.
6. Now try again using any 10 Geoshapes. Make sure that you both have the same shapes and colours to start with.
7. Make a list of the most helpful language that you and your partner used.

© 3D GEOSHAPES 1995

Tunnel Vision

Strand and Objectives

Space
- build structures and make geometric models, analysing their cross-sections and nets

Measurement
- measure, compare and order objects and events using length, capacity, mass, area, volume, time and angle
- choose appropriate units for tasks by considering purpose, and the need for precision and/or communication

Attitudes
- show a positive response to the use of mathematics as a tool in practical situations
- display a willingness and ability to work cooperatively with others and to value the contribution of others

Number
- recognise, produce and use patterns in number

Algebra
- make and use arithmetic generalisations

Mathematical Inquiry
- observe, represent and extend spatial and number patterns
- explain conjectures and results, using appropriate mathematical language

Duration   60 minutes
Group size   8 children working in 2 groups of 4
Materials
58 triangles and 75 squares

1. This activity works well in a theme on Transport.
2. The rules for tunnel building ensure that the two groups will make the same length tunnels. Group 1 makes a tunnel which is 15 sets of open ended cubes, each with a square as the base. Group 2 makes a tunnel which is 15 sets of open ended square pyramids linked by triangles. Each section of this tunnel also has a square as the base. Group 2 may produce the square pyramid based tunnel rotated around its long axis so that triangles are on the floor, but it could be argued that this is not the longest possible tunnel.
3. Both tunnels will cover the same area as they both have 15 squares in the base.
4. The weight of the two tunnels can be found by measuring the weight of one Geoshape square and one Geoshape triangle and multiplying by the number of each used in the tunnel construction. However,

© 3D GEOSHAPES 1995

school measuring equipment may not be accurate enough to measure the weight of one Geoshape piece. Therefore it will be necessary to weigh an appropriate part of the tunnel and multiply.

5. The cube based tunnel, being larger, usually allows quicker passage of the pen and the ruler, but dexterity and teamwork also come into play.
6. You may wish to ask the children about the volume of each tunnel. The children should be able to tell you by observation that the volume of the cube based tunnel is much larger.
7. Vocabulary that you could encourage the children to be using with you and with each other includes: *length, mass, area, volume, compare, difference, estimate, calculate, time, hundredths of seconds, base, grams, millimetres ...*
8. Assessment of the activity by observation allows you to note:
    - cooperation in the building of the tunnel
    - skills and strategies used in solving problems
    - leadership qualities displayed
    - initiative displayed by individuals or the group
    - accuracy of estimations

Follow-up Ideas

1. The timing experiment can be extended by holding the two tunnels so that the passed object moves under the influence of gravity. The tunnels can be vertical, or the square pyramid based construction could be held so its missing triangle face is on the floor. This causes the tunnel to slant like the Leaning Tower of Pisa and also suggests experiments based on dropping the vertical distance from the top of the tower, or sliding down the channel formed on the inside where the triangle 'walls' meet. Ball bearings are useful in this experiment.
2. Which tunnel is stronger? Why? Conduct a strength test using weights placed on the roof of each tunnel or by applying pressure at both ends of the tunnel. The square based pyramid tunnel should prove far stronger than the cube based one, because of the triangles in its construction.
3. Explore the number of pieces needed to construct each tunnel. Each group can investigate the number of pieces for a tunnel with 1, 2, 3, 4, 5, squares in the base and then predict for tunnels with 20, 50, 100, n squares in the base. The data collected in this investigation can be stored in a table, graphed, or entered in a spreadsheet which links the tabulated values to a graph.
4. Challenge the children to design and make a tunnel with a curve in it.

Tunnel Vision

1. Group 1 uses 60 squares and Group 2 uses 15 squares and 58 triangles. The challenge is for each group to build the longest possible tunnel. Before constructing the tunnels, try to work out which tunnel will be the longer. Write down how you worked out your guess.

2. Rules for building tunnels
   - Use *only* the Geoshape pieces given.
   - Tunnels must sit flat on the floor the whole way.
   - Tunnels must be joined the whole way along top, bottom and sides.
   - Group 1 must build a rectangular tunnel.

3. Compare your tunnels:
   - Which tunnel is longer? Why?
   - Which tunnel covers more area of the floor? How did you work this out?
   - Which tunnel weighs more? How can you work this out without putting the whole tunnel on the scales?
   - Work out the time it takes to pass a pen from one end of your tunnel to the other. Which is faster? Why? Now try with a 30 cm ruler.

Useful Machines

TEACHERS' NOTES

Strand and Objectives

Attitudes
- show a positive response to the use of mathematics as a tool in practical situations

Space
- build structures and make geometric models, analysing their cross-sections and nets

Mathematical Inquiry
- use personal and group organisational skills to help in tackling mathematical problems

Duration   40 minutes
Group size   3 or 4 children
Materials
Geoshapes, clever sticks, cotton wool, pop sticks, pipe-cleaners, paper, elastic bands, and other construction materials

1. It is a good idea to begin this activity with a brainstorm of ideas for machines, eg: sausage making machines, an automatic pencil case or an automatic head scratcher.
2. The group's machine must have a purpose. This purpose and the design features which complement it are the focus of a final report which can be either written or oral.
3. Encourage a planning stage of drawings to indicate how the machine will be made.
4. This activity provides a good opportunity to observe cooperative skills and make anecdotal records.

Follow-up Ideas
1. Construct and describe:
    - a robot making machine
    - an alien who is your friend
    - a mouse trap
    - a rocket

© 3D GEOSHAPES 1995

Useful Machines

1. As a group think of a machine you would like to make. It must have a purpose.
2. Draw sketches to show how you will make your machine with Geoshapes.

3. Make the machine.
4. Prepare a report explaining the purpose of your machine and the features of its design which help it achieve the purpose.

The Three Bears

TEACHERS' NOTES

Strand and Objectives

Measurement
- choose appropriate units for tasks by considering purpose, and the need for precision and/or communication

Attitudes
- demonstrate the confidence to apply mathematics and to gain knowledge about mathematics
- display a willingness and ability to work cooperatively with others and to value the contribution of others

Space
- build structures and make geometric models, analysing their cross-sections and nets

Mathematical Inquiry
- use personal and group organisational skills to help in tackling mathematical problems

Duration 60 minutes plus follow-up sessions
Group size 3 children
Materials
Assorted Geoshapes and art materials

1. This activity is time consuming, but because of its cross-curricular nature (maths, art, technology, language) it can be used in conjunction with scheduled times such as art.
2. You may like to allocate each group a piece of furniture and then make an area where all the furniture is placed together to make the three bears' house.
3. Allow children freedom to use other materials for decoration. For example, some children might like to make a mattress out of cotton wool and pillows out of decorated matchboxes.

Follow-up Ideas

1. Make dog kennels for three different sized dogs, eg: German Shepherd, Blue Heeler and Poodle. Make the dogs from playdoh or other modelling material, then put them in the kennels.

© 3D GEOSHAPES 1995

The Three Bears

1. In your group, choose one piece of furniture and make it three times in three different sizes for Father Bear, Mother Bear and Baby Bear. You must keep the same design, but change the size to suit the three different bears.
   Here are some suggestions:
   beds, chairs, tables, wardrobes, bookshelves, dressing tables, bedside tables, lamps, stools.

2. After you have made your furniture, make the three bears out of cardboard. Remember to measure carefully because your bears need to match the furniture.

3. If there is time left you can repeat the task for a different piece of furniture.

4. You may like to decorate your furniture by adding material, paper, pop sticks, wool or anything else you can think of. By doing this you are using your Geoshapes as a frame.

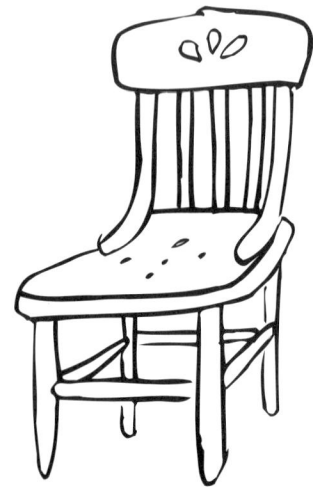

© 3D GEOSHAPES 1995

Dream Home

TEACHERS' NOTES

Strand and Objectives

Space
- build structures and make geometric models, analysing their cross-sections and nets
- compare and classify objects, analyse their shapes and describe in conventional geometric language
- interpret and produce two-dimensional representations of objects

Choosing and Using Mathematics
- clarify and pose problems arising in practical or imagined contexts

Attitudes
- show a positive response to the use of mathematics as a tool in practical situations
- show an awareness that creativity and initiative are encouraged and valued within mathematics education

Mathematical Inquiry
- use personal and group organisational skills to help in tackling mathematical problems

Duration 30 - 45 minutes
Group size 6 children working in pairs
Materials
30 triangles, 30 squares, and 4 pentagons per pair

1. Encourage children to consider the Geoshape pieces they are required to use when sketching the designs of their houses.
2. Continually ask children to justify their models by asking questions such as: *Why did you use the pentagons like this? What is this room for? Could you make your model a two-storey one? Why not?*
3. When all the houses are finished compare them and ask children to explain the design features. Ensure that there are no curious bits that appear to be simply tacked on because the pair did not know what else to do with them. If there are add-ons the pair should attempt to explain them. eg: *This is an outside gate. This is a solar panel in the roof.* Encourage the class to ask questions and observe the presenters' ability to respond to these. Make notes of the children's explanations and their ability to justify their designs.
4. Vocabulary that you could encourage the children to use with you and with each other includes: *construct, design, lay-out, pentagon, structure, surface, cube, interior, exterior, model, area, space, cross-section ...*

© 3D GEOSHAPES 1995

TEACHERS' NOTES

Dream Home

Follow-up Ideas

1. This activity can be extended to have each pair consider additional aspects of their model. eg:
   - the materials they would use to construct a real house based on their Geoshape model and why they would choose these materials
   - the colour scheme they would use for the interior or exterior
2. Using their models as the basis, have children decide on an interior layout for their dream home. eg:
   This would be the kitchen; this room would have the indoor pool and revolving dance floor in it.
   These layouts could be represented using a bird's eye view of the house, ie: looking down into the house through the roof and ceiling
3. Ask children if they can break their construction along the Geoshape joins to form a cross-section of their home.
4. Each pair writes a design brief for another pair to follow. eg:
   The house has to be over 20 cm tall, it must have an inside pool in the shape of a pentagon, it must have a front and back door that can swing open ...

© 3D GEOSHAPES 1995

Dream Home

In this activity you work with a partner to make a dream home. However all architects and builders must follow rules and regulations and so must you. These are your rules and regulations.

- You must use all of your Geoshape pieces - 30 triangles, 30 squares and 4 pentagons.
- You must sketch a design of what you hope your house will end up looking like.
- Your house must be able to stand up by itself.
- Your house must have a sloping roof.
- Your house must have a garage that is attached to the main building.
- You must include a bathroom that is built inside your house - the size and shape of the bathroom is up to you.
- Your house can include any other rooms or features that you like, but you will need to be able to explain them.

TEACHERS' NOTES

Weak or Strong?

Strand and Objectives

Space
- compare and classify objects, analyse their shapes and describe in conventional geometric language

Choosing and Using Mathematics
- clarify and pose problems arising in practical or imagined contexts

Measurement
- measure, compare and order objects and events using length, capacity, mass, area, volume, time and angle

Mathematical Inquiry
- test conjectures in space and number and search for counter-examples
- explain conjectures and results, using appropriate mathematical language
- undertake structured investigations, individually and collaboratively

Duration   30 minutes

Group size   10 children working in pairs

Materials

20 triangles, 30 squares, 5 pentagons and two 1 kg weights per pair

1. This activity has links to:
   - science: testing hypotheses, conducting experiments, drawing conclusions
   - technology: shape, strength, rigidity
   - language: recording results, writing conclusions, presenting reports
2. Before beginning testing, children should ensure that all the Geoshapes are correctly joined.
3. Encourage the children to apply pressure gradually when testing the polyhedra. Depending on the shape of the construction, some will collapse with little pressure while others will stand considerably more before collapsing.
4. In question 2 of Activity B, either bagged or metal 1 kg weights can be used for testing the strength of the polyhedra. Some of the polyhedra may need to be held steady against a solid surface while weights are applied. It may be an idea to have some 500g and 250g masses to develop a more gradually increasing strength test.

Weak or Strong?

TEACHERS' NOTES

5. Vocabulary that you could encourage the children to be using with you and with each other includes: *polyhedron, net, square base, edge, face, corner, surface, prism, triangular prism, rectangular prism, tetrahedron, strong, strength, weak, rigid, flexible, cube, pyramid ...*
6. Examples of the type of tests children may design in question 3 of Activity B are:
   - dropping the tetrahedron from one metre, then dropping each of the other models from the same height onto the same surface. The drop height can be varied.
   - attaching string to the sides of the model, placing the model in the centre of a table, dangling the string over the edges, attaching weights to the string and gradually increasing the weight.
   - testing to find the maximum weight a model can lift from various points on its structure.
   - dropping progressively larger weights onto the models from a designated height.
7. Have each pair write a report (point form, not narrative). The report should include the test conducted, how they reached their conclusions from the results, drawings and diagrams and final opinions on why some polyhedra are stronger, more rigid or more flexible than others.

Follow-up Ideas
1. Make a larger version of one model and test its strength. eg: Turn the 5 piece square pyramid into a 20 piece version with 4 squares as the base and 16 triangles. Test, and explain what happens.
2. Take the children on a walk around the school and local neighbourhood and identify where triangles, tetrahedrons, triangular prisms, squares, cubes, rectangles, rectangular prisms, ... are used. Magazine pictures of a range of structures also complement this task.
3. Repeat Activity B using the *Geoshape Geodesic Dome*. This is available as a separate kit.

© 3D GEOSHAPES 1995

Weak or Strong? A

1. Make a cube and a tetrahedron. Hold each one in turn between your hands and squeeze gently. Gradually increase the force of your squeeze until the object begins to break apart.
Which is the stronger? Why? Why not?

2. Try the experiment again with each of these *polyhedra*:
   - square pyramid

   - rectangular prism

   - triangular prism

   - any 3D object of your choice

3. As a group try to place the polyhedra you have tested in order from strongest to weakest. Discuss questions like:
   - Which polyhedron was strongest?
   - Is the square pyramid stronger than the cube?
   - Is the triangular prism stronger than the rectangular one?

4. Record your results.

Weak or Strong? B

1. Make at least two of these polyhedra.

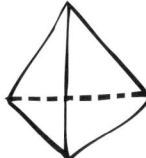 

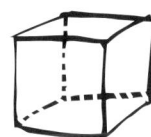  

2. Place a 1 kilogram mass on each, to test their strength. What happened? If they didn't collapse, try doing the same with 2 kilograms.
Which polyhedra collapse? Why? Which are the strongest? Why?

3. Think up a test of your own to apply to these polyhedra.

4. Write a report about your experiments.

TEACHERS' NOTES

Fill in the Shape

Strand and Objectives

Measurement ... area

- measure, compare and order objects and events using length, capacity, mass, area, volume, time and angle

Attitudes

- exhibit a willingness to persist when solving problems and to try different methods of attack

Space

- compare and classify figures, analyse their shapes and describe in conventional geometric language

Duration 30 minutes

Group size Pairs

Materials

12 assorted Geoshapes and large butchers' paper per child

1. Children will need large paper as 12 Geoshapes can cover a lot of area.
2. If a child is having difficulty recreating their partner's shape from the outline, you might allow the clue of knowing which shapes were used to make the design.
3. This activity is useful in a mixed ability class because the quicker workers continue to swap with each other, while the slower ones are pondering their drawings.
4. Collect suitable examples of the children's drawings and laminate them for future use.

Follow-up Ideas

1. On butchers' paper, draw free hand any closed shape. Cover it with a Geoshape grid. Where the Geoshapes go over the edges, trace around the part of the Geoshapes which stick out. Swap drawings and try to remake the Geoshape grid.
2. Repeat Follow-up 1 using only one type of Geoshape. The designer specifies on the drawing the number and type of Geoshapes used.

© 3D GEOSHAPES 1995

Fill in the Shape

1. Make a flat, connected 2D shape from 6 Geoshapes.
2. Place your shape onto some butchers' paper and carefully trace around the outside edge only, then take your shape apart.

3. Give your tracing to your partner and ask them to remake the shape.
4. Repeat the same activity using 7, 10 and 12 Geoshapes.

TEACHERS' NOTES

Tile the Table

Strand and Objectives

Space

- recognise congruent figures by superimposition, and informally investigate congruent figures
- rearrange, fit together and tessellate figures and stack and pack objects

Mathematical Inquiry

- observe, represent and extend spatial and number patterns
- test conjectures in space and number and search for counter-examples

Duration   20 minutes
Group size   8 children working in pairs
Materials
20 triangles, 15 squares, 8 pentagons and 9 hexagons per pair

1. The squares and the triangles and many combinations of both will tessellate very well as do the hexagons. However the pentagons do not form a pattern by themselves. Even using pentagons with squares and triangles no tessellation can be formed.

2. Vocabulary that you could encourage the children to use with you and with each other includes: *tessellation, congruent, non-congruent, tiling, surface ...*

3. Tessellation work may be linked to art and also to symmetry work. Look around the school, local shopping centre and the children's homes for examples of tessellations. What shapes are used? Are they congruent? How is the pattern made. eg:

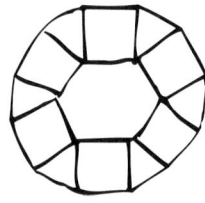

4. Use children's drawings of their tessellations to gather assessment information. If the drawings are filed, notes may be made directly onto the examples. eg:
   - knows and identifies congruent shapes
   - can tessellate with more than one shape
   - creates aesthetic patterns to cover a given area

20

© 3D GEOSHAPES 1995

Tile the Table

TEACHERS' NOTES

Follow-up Ideas

1. Ask the children to take 4 Geoshape squares and make as many different 2D shapes with these as possible. eg:

   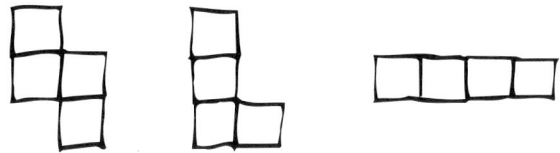

   These shapes are called tetrominoes. There are 5 possible shapes.
   Ask the children the following questions:
   Which of these tetrominoes are symmetrical?
   Which tetrominoes look the same when you turn them 90 degrees?
   Which tetrominoes tessellate?

2. Ask children to make a tessellation using:
   - hexagons and squares
   - hexagons, squares and triangles

   Do these shape combinations tessellate?

© 3D GEOSHAPES 1995

Tile the Table

1. Work with a partner to tile some of your table with either squares *or* triangles.
   Tiling a flat surface in a repeating pattern with no overlapping shapes and no gaps between the shapes is called tessellating.

2. Try tessellating using squares *and* triangles. Draw the pattern you have made.

3. Try tessellating using:
   - pentagons
   - pentagons and squares
   - pentagons and triangles
   - hexagons

   Discuss your tessellations with other groups.

4. Do hexagons tessellate better than the pentagons? Why? Why not?

5. Create other tessellations by combining shapes.

6. Draw the different tessellations you create.

Finding Volumes

TEACHERS' NOTES

Strand and Objectives

Space
- build structures and make geometric models, analysing their cross-sections and nets
- rearrange, fit together and tessellate figures and stack and pack objects

Measurement ...volume
- measure, compare and order objects and events using length, capacity, mass, area, volume, time and angle
- choose appropriate units for tasks by considering purpose, and the need for precision and/or communication

Mathematical Inquiry
- test conjectures in space and number and search for counter-examples

Duration 45 - 60 minutes
Group size 6 children
Materials
96 squares per group

1. In Activity A question 4, children use 24 squares to make a cube. In Activity B question 1, children use 54 squares, and the final cube, the *mega-cube*, requires 96 squares.
2. Vocabulary that you could encourage the children to use with you and each other includes: *2D, two-dimensional, 3D, three-dimensional, cube, volume, area, space, faces, length, width, height, construct...*
3. The written reports of the activities could be done individually, or alternatively be prepared by the group who then nominate two people to present to the class. The reports could include a model and drawings of the cubes they constructed during the session. They might also comment on how well, or otherwise, the members of the group worked together.

© 3D GEOSHAPES 1995

TEACHERS' NOTES

Finding Volumes

Follow-up Ideas

1. Challenge children to predict how many squares would be needed to make the next largest cube after the *mega-cube* and the one after that. Encourage them to look for a pattern in the number of squares needed to make the progressively larger cubes.

2. Provide the children with some larger cartons and boxes. Using 6-square Geoshape cubes, have them calculate the volume of these boxes. eg:
   Volume of box 1 = 16 Geoshape cubes with some space left over.
   Did the Geoshape cubes work well for this. Why? Why not?

3. Try some backwards questions. eg:
   I have 598 Geoshape squares. Will I be able to use them all to exactly make a cube?
   or,
   Which of these numbers of Geoshape squares would exactly make a cube?
      10   16   24   48   60   96   100   150

4. Have the children compare a cube made from 6 squares to a cubic centimetre (centicube or MAB 10 mini). Use some cubic centimetres to work out the volume of a 6-square Geoshape cube? What is the volume in cubic centimetres of a 24-square Geoshape cube?

5. Make up any complete 3D shape using 24 squares then try and work out what the volume of this shape is in cubic centimetres.

© 3D GEOSHAPES 1995

Finding Volumes A

* Volume is the amount of space inside a 3D object.
Cubes can be used to measure volume. *

1. Share 96 squares evenly between the group.
2. Each person use 6 squares to make a cube.
3. With a partner from your group, *guess first* and then count the number of cubes of this size it would take to fill:
    - your locker tub
    - your school bag
    - a section of a cupboard
    - a row of a bookshelf
    - two other things you choose

4. In two groups of three, make the next biggest cube. With this size cube, guess first and then measure the volume of two things.
5. Write a report of your volume investigations.

Finding Volumes B

* Volume is the amount of space inside a 3D object. Cubes can be used to measure volume. *

1. As one group of six make a cube which has 9 squares in each face. Use this cube to find the volume of the space under a table and the volume of two other things you choose.

2. Now make a cube which has 16 squares in each face. Guess first and then try to measure the volume of your room with this *mega-cube*.

3. Write a report of your volume investigations.

Stack 'em & Pack 'em

TEACHERS' NOTES

Strand and Objectives

Space

- compare and classify objects, analyse their shapes and describe in conventional geometric language
- rearrange, fit together and tessellate figures and stack and pack objects

Mathematical Inquiry

- test conjectures in space and number and search for counter-examples

Duration 30 minutes

Group size 4 children

Materials

80 triangles, 80 squares, 60 pentagons and a range of empty cardboard boxes of various sizes.

1. Emphasise the need for the children to hypothesise whether each of the polyhedra will stack or pack readily or not, and why, before actually testing them. Ask children why they have designated a certain shape as being unsuitable for stacking or packing. What features of the shape caused the problem? Conversely, what features make a shape suitable? Were some of the polyhedra that were nominated as good for stacking, also nominated as good for packing?

2. In Activity A, children should come to appreciate that certain shapes will stack more readily than others. Of the eight polyhedra they have been asked to make there are some that will stack easily, the cube, triangular prism and rectangular prism; some that will stack satisfactorily but with some rearranging, the tetrahedron, square pyramid and pentagonal prism; and some that are more unsuitable for stacking, the octahedron and dodecahedron. Encourage the children to experiment with different stacking arrangements when testing each shape, turning shapes on their side, flipping others over and stacking back to back, can all add to the 'stackability' of an object.

3. In Activity B, you will need to provide children with a range of boxes to test their notions about which polyhedra pack readily. Encourage children to talk about polyhedra leaving no gaps, or small gaps, and anything else they notice. Were there any surprises?

© 3D GEOSHAPES 1995

TEACHERS' NOTES

Stack 'em & Pack 'em

4. Vocabulary that you could encourage the children to be using with you and with each other includes: *cube, tetrahedron, pentagon, pentagonal prism, triangular prism, square pyramid, octahedron, rectangular prism, stack, prism, vertical, arrange, rearrange, predict, test ...*

5. Stacking and packing are readily observable and useful examples of the practical application of mathematical knowledge and concepts.

6. Listening to the group's explanations of why they have filled in their tables as they have, will provide assessment information on their knowledge of stacking and packing qualities. It will also provide process information on how well the group worked together and reached decisions.

Follow-up Ideas

1. Take the children on a visit to a local supermarket or department store and have them note the way products are stacked and packed. Do cylinders stack well? Why? What sort of cartons are used for packing light objects? Why are small cartons used for packing heavy items? What is the most common shape used in stacking displays? Ask them to draw some of the displays highlighting how various items are stacked.

© 3D GEOSHAPES 1995

Stack 'em & Pack 'em A

cube 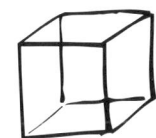   tetrahedron

square pyramid    rectangular prism

triangular prism    pentagonal prism

octahedron    dodecahedron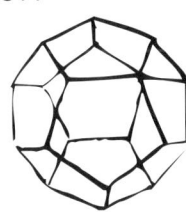

1. The 3D objects above are called *polyhedra*. As a group, decide which of these polyhedra would be *good*, *average* or *not good* for stacking. Record your reasons.

2. Now consider one polyhedron at a time and make several copies of it to test your decisions. Fill in this table.

	Good	Average	Not good
1. cube			
2. tetrahedron			
3. square pyramid			
4. rectangular prism			
5. triangular prism			
6. pentagonal prism			
7. octahedron			
8. dodecahedron			

© 3D GEOSHAPES 1995

Stack 'em & Pack 'em B

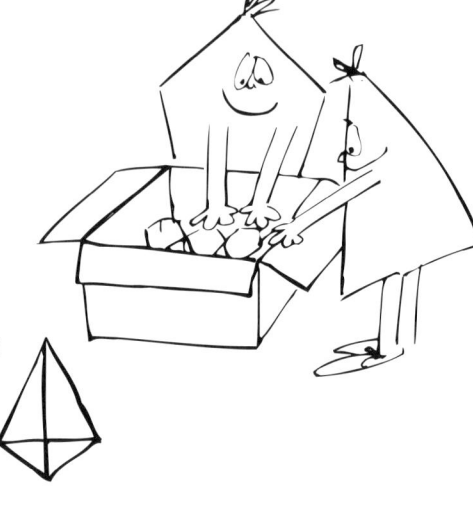

cube    tetrahedron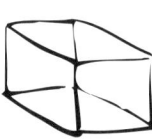

square pyramid    rectangular prism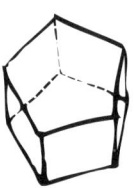

triangular prism 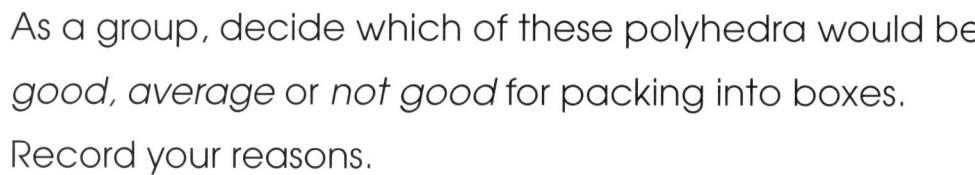   pentagonal prism

octahedron    dodecahedron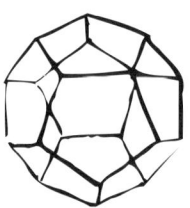

1. The 3D objects above are called polyhedra. As a group, decide which of these polyhedra would be *good, average* or *not good* for packing into boxes. Record your reasons.

2. Now consider one polyhedron at a time and make several copies of it to test your decisions. Fill in this table.

	Good	Average	Not good
1. cube			
2. tetrahedron			
3. square pyramid			
4. rectangular prism			
5. triangular prism			
6. pentagonal prism			
7. octahedron			
8. dodecahedron			

© 3D GEOSHAPES 1995

Four Room Apartments

TEACHERS' NOTES

Strand and Objectives

Space
- build structures and make geometric models, analysing their cross-sections and nets
- rearrange, fit together and tessellate figures and stack and pack objects
- interpret and produce two-dimensional representations of objects
- plan and execute arrangements according to specifications

Mathematical Inquiry
- test conjectures in space and number and search for counter-examples
- undertake structured investigations, individually and collaboratively

Duration   30 - 40 minutes

Group size   Pairs

Materials

24 squares per pair

1. The cubes used for this activity are made of 6 Geoshape squares. They will stack on top of or beside each other, but they will not attach to each other.
2. When demonstrating the rules for stacking the cubes, discuss what an aerial view of the stack arrangement would look like. Discuss the meaning of the numbers with the children. eg: 2 denotes 2 storeys.
Explore other suggestions the children may make to record the aerial view.
3. Question 5 in the activity, *How do you know if you have found them all?*, implies organising the solutions and arguing that there can be no more.
4. Aerial views of possible solutions:

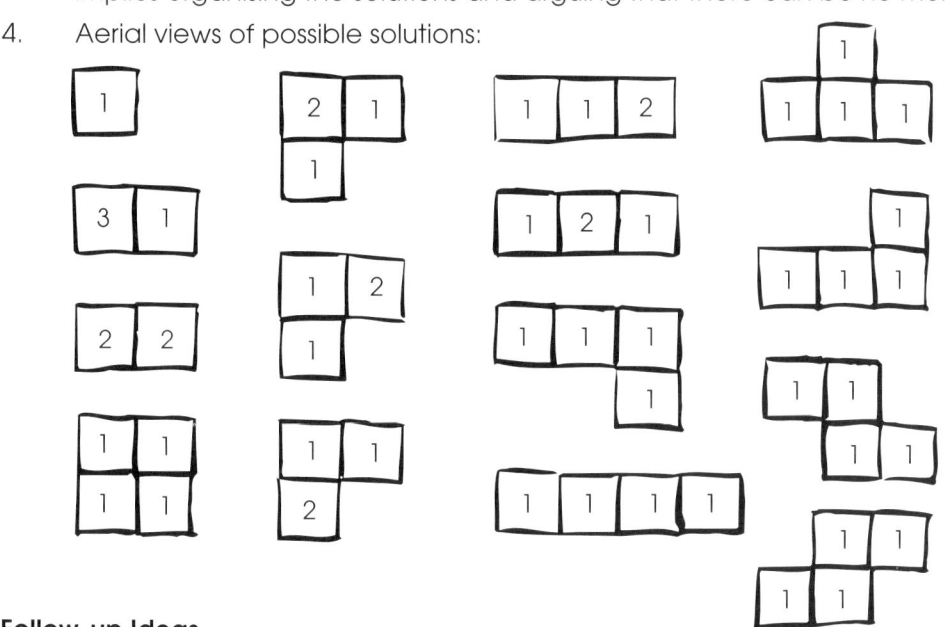

Follow-up Ideas

1. Work together as a class to make a rich person's village.
2. What four room apartments can be made if the rules are not followed?
3. What three room or five room apartments can be made?

© 3D GEOSHAPES 1995

Four Room Apartments

1. Use 24 squares to make four cubes.
2. A rich person wants to build a village of apartments with four rooms. Each apartment must have a different room arrangement and obey these rules:

    - Faces and edges of the rooms must all touch fully.

    - If one apartment can be rotated on the block of land to become another, then the two arrangements are not considered different.
    eg: These are both the same and only one can be used.

    - Colour doesn't matter.
3. Build as many different apartment plans as you can. Sketch an aerial view of each one.
4. Show some of your sketches to a classmate to see if they can build your four room apartments.
5. How many apartment plans are possible?
   How do you know when you have found them all?

View It Carefully!

TEACHERS' NOTES

Strand and Objectives

Space

- interpret and produce two-dimensional representations of objects
- plan and execute arrangements according to specifications

Duration 45 minutes +

Group size Pairs

Materials

12 triangles, 6 squares and 2 pentagons per pair

1. For this activity it will be necessary to demonstrate drawing front and aerial views for a simple model first. Point out to the children that even though connected sides form two lines, they are shown in the drawings as one because they are directly behind each other. Also point out that a dotted line means the line is at the back, but it is drawn in because it can be seen through the structure.
2. Shapes 4 and 5 on the activity sheet are quite sophisticated and you may prefer to reserve these for extension work.

Follow-up Ideas

1. Children create their own simple model and draw the front and aerial views. Drawings can be given to another child to see if they can make the model from the drawing.

© 3D GEOSHAPES 1995

View It Carefully!

The pictures below show the *front view* and *aerial view* of five Geoshape constructions.

Make each one using the information given.

                        front view   aerial view

1. 3 squares.

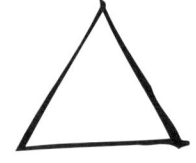

2. 1 square
   4 triangles.

3. 5 squares
   4 triangles.

4. 6 squares
   12 triangles.

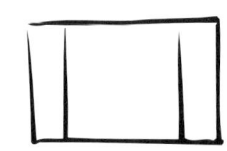

5. 5 squares
   2 pentagons.

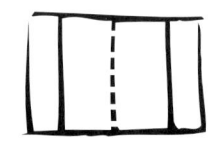

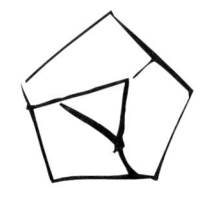

© 3D GEOSHAPES 1995

Tetrahedron Nets

TEACHERS' NOTES

Strand and Objectives

Space

- build structures and make geometric models, analysing their cross-sections and nets
- carry out rotations, translations and reflections and recognise and produce related symmetries
- recognise congruent figures by superimposition, and informally investigate congruent figures
- interpret and produce two-dimensional representations of objects

Duration 15 - 30 minutes

Group size Pairs

Materials

8 triangles (4 colours x 2) per pair

1. If the children are having trouble with the task you might ask:
   Have you tried unhinging the bottom first?

2. The second net is:

3. The two different tetrahedrons in question 5 are mirror images of each other. To make these, first make two tetrahedron nets with the colours as mirror images.

Follow-up Ideas

1. Use the activity *How Many Triangles?*
2. Use the activity *Stack 'em & Pack 'em*.

© 3D GEOSHAPES 1995

Tetrahedron Nets

1. Make a tetrahedron using 4 different coloured triangles. *Tetra is Greek for 4*

2. Unfold the tetrahedron into a flat net like this:

3. Refold the tetrahedron. Then unfold it again so that a different colour is in the middle.
   Repeat this until you have made each colour be in the middle.

4. There is a different shaped net which makes a tetrahedron. Can you find it?

5. Using the four different coloured triangles in each tetrahedron, make 2 tetrahedrons which are *not identical* to each other.

Adapted from the Mathematics Task Centre Project and used with permission of Curriculum Corporation.

Cube Nets

TEACHERS' NOTES

Strand and Objectives

Space
- build structures and make geometric models, analysing their cross-sections and nets
- interpret and produce two-dimensional representations of objects

Choosing and Using Mathematics
- choose and use mathematical skills to make decisions
- clarify and pose problems arising in practical or imagined contexts
- verify and interpret solutions with respect to the original problem

Duration 30 - 45 minutes

Group size Pairs

Materials

12 squares per pair

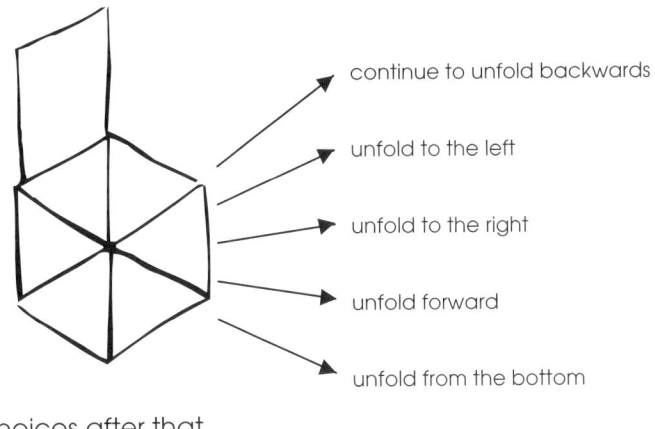

1. Most children will stick at this task until they find all eleven nets. For some though it may be useful to explore the problem as follows:
   For the first unfold, all edges are the same. In other words, it doesn't matter where you start. Choices after that might be represented in a diagram like the one above:
   Each of these choices leads to other choices, which eventually leads to all possible nets.

   - continue to unfold backwards
   - unfold to the left
   - unfold to the right
   - unfold forward
   - unfold from the bottom

2. The eleven solutions are:

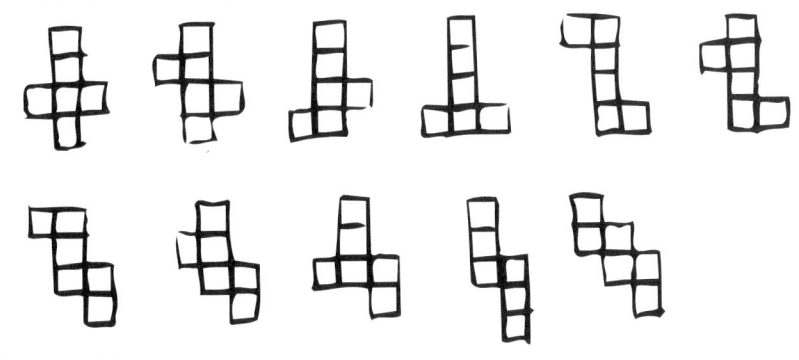

Follow-up Ideas

1. A hexomino is a 2D shape made by joining 6 squares by their edges. How many hexominoes exist? Use the material supplied with the task, or draw on graph paper, to find all 35. Making and testing all the 35 to see which ones will fold to make a cube is another way of finding the 11 nets of a cube.

© 3D GEOSHAPES 1995

Cube Nets

A net is a flat shape that will fold up to make a 3D object.

This net folds up to make a cube:

1. Join 6 squares to make a cube. Try to unfold it to make a net like the one in the picture above.

2. Remake the cube and try to unfold it into a different shaped net. Here are three:

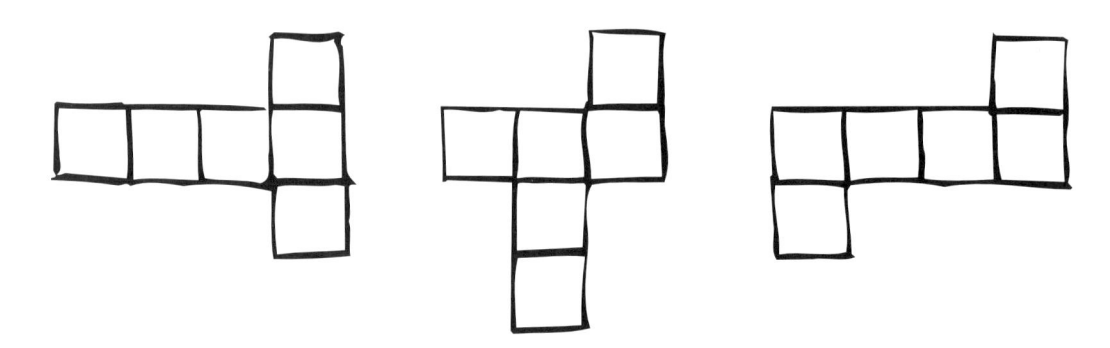

3. There are actually eleven different nets. Keep making and unfolding the cube in different ways to find all of them. Make a drawing of each one.

Adapted from the Mathematics Task Centre Project and used with permission of Curriculum Corporation.

Nets, Pyramids and Prisms

TEACHERS' NOTES

Strand and Objectives

Space

- build structures and make geometric models, analysing their cross-sections and nets
- interpret and produce two-dimensional representations of objects

Choosing and Using Mathematics

- choose and use mathematical skills to make decisions
- verify and interpret solutions with respect to the original problem

Duration   30 - 45 minutes

Group size   10 children working in pairs

Materials

15 triangles, 25 squares and 1 pentagon per pair

1. This activity works best if used after the activities Tetrahedron Nets and Cube Nets. If used this way, the first two objects on the activity sheet will have already been investigated.

2. Encourage the children to make observations such as:
   Our prism has a triangle at both ends.
   When you have a triangular pyramid it doesn't matter which way you put it down.

3. Question 2 in the activity, *How do you know if you have found them all?*, implies organising the solutions and arguing that there can be no more.

4. Vocabulary that you could encourage the children to use with you and with each other includes: *net, square, edge, face, corner, surface, parallel, pyramid, prism, triangular prism ...*

5. One method of assessing this activity is to have one pair make an object (limited to perhaps 12 assorted Geoshape pieces and not seen by the other children) and then show this completed shape to another pair. The second pair uses the same type and colour pieces to make the net of the object without breaking apart the original object. Observe this activity and record assessment information.

© 3D GEOSHAPES 1995

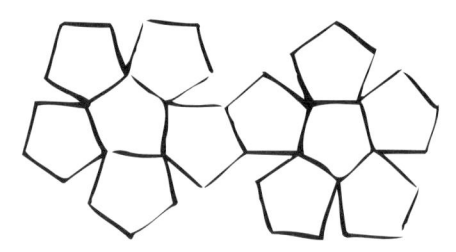

Nets, Pyramids and Prisms

TEACHERS' NOTES

Follow-up Ideas

1. As children make each of their pyramids or prisms, have them identify the faces, edges and corners of the objects.
2. Ask each pair to count and record the number of faces and edges for each pyramid and prism that they construct, eg: a square pyramid has 5 faces and 8 edges, a triangular prism has 5 faces and 9 edges.
3. Challenge the children to make the net for an *octahedron*. This is made of 8 triangles and looks like this:

   This is the net

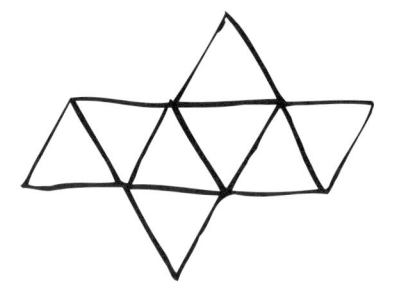

4. Challenge the children to make the net for a *dodecahedron*. This is made of 12 pentagons and looks like this:

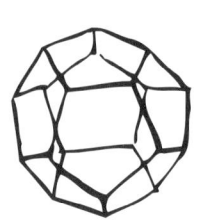

   This is the net

© 3D GEOSHAPES 1995

Nets, Pyramids and Prisms

A *net* is a flat shape that will fold up to make a 3D object.

A *pyramid* has one point on top and different shape bases. A *prism* has the same shape base and top and every other face is rectangular.

1. Work with a partner to make nets for each of these objects:
    - triangular pyramid
    - square prism
    - square pyramid
    - triangular prism
    - rectangular prism
    - pentagular pyramid
2. How many nets can be made for each object?
   How do you know when you have found them all?
3. Draw each net.

Shape Sketch

TEACHERS' NOTES

Strand and Objectives

Space

- compare and classify objects, analyse their shapes and describe in conventional geometric language
- interpret and produce two-dimensional representations of objects

Duration 45 - 60 minutes

Group size 8 children working in pairs

Materials

10 triangles, 25 squares, 2 pentagons, a thin blacklead pencil, white paper or dotted isometric grid paper and eraser per pair

1. This activity fosters the ability to sketch 3D objects. Making the objects with Geoshapes allows the children to look inside the object and appreciate its depth as well as its length and width. This assists in working out what edges are at the back and would normally not be seen if the shape was enclosed or covered. It is these edges that are represented by dotted lines, giving the impression of the sketch being three-dimensional.

2. If children are experiencing difficulty with sketching, the dotted isometric grid paper at the back of this book may prove useful in helping them plan and outline the 3D object they are attempting to sketch.

3. Vocabulary that you could encourage the children to be using with you and with each other includes: *view, viewpoints, three-dimensional, 3D, two-dimensional, 2D, pyramid, square pyramid, tetrahedron, cube, rectangular prism, triangular prism, pentagonal prism, cylinder ...*

4. The skills developed in this activity can readily be transferred to many art activities where sketching of 3D objects is involved. Conversely, if the children have developed skills in the use of shading during art sessions, this can be effectively used to accentuate the three-dimensional aspect of their sketches.

© 3D GEOSHAPES 1995

Shape Sketch

TEACHERS' NOTES

5. Collecting completed or rough sketches as samples of work can provide you with an accurate idea of how well the children performed. You may wish to make observations or notes directly onto the sample concerning their ability to represent three dimensions on a 2D medium. You may also choose to interview each pair of children as you are viewing their work. Possible interview questions are:

   How did you manage to do this working as a pair. Who did what?
   Why is this edge represented by dotted lines?
   Did you find this easy or difficult? Why?
   How many tries did it take you to get to this final sketch?
   Are you happy with it? Why? Why Not?

   It may be appropriate to take brief notes of their replies and comments and include these with your anecdotal records.

Follow-up Ideas

1. Point of View

   Using the same 3D objects, ask each pair to draw a top view of each shape. eg:

   Top view of a square pyramid   Top view of a triangular prism

   After completing a top view sketch for each of the six objects, pairs could swap their views with another and try to match the sketches with the objects.

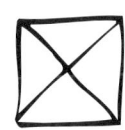

2. Repeat this activity for side views.

© 3D GEOSHAPES 1995

Shape Sketch A

1. Work with a partner to make these polyhedra:

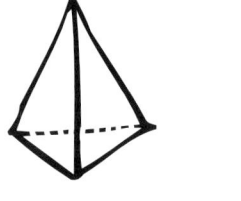

   tetrahedron 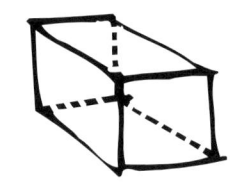   rectangular prism    pentagonal prism

2. Look at these objects from the front, from above, and from each side. Talk to your partner about the features of each of your models. eg:
   - What's special about a tetrahedron?
   - How many faces does a rectangular prism have?
   - What shapes make a pentagonal prism?

3. The dotted lines are used to make the shape look like it has depth as well as length and width. They show edges which are at the back and would not be seen if the object was solid.
   Find the parts which the dotted lines represent.

Shape Sketch B

1. Work with a partner to make these polyhedra:
   - cube
   - square pyramid
   - triangular prism

2. Here are sketches of two other polyhedra.

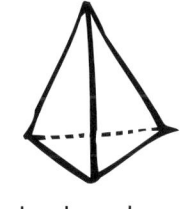

   tetrahedron 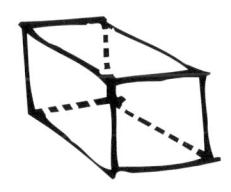   rectangular prism

   See how the dotted lines are used to show the edges that are at the back of the object.

3. Copy the way the tetrahedron and rectangular prism are drawn, then try sketching the polyhedra you have made.

TEACHERS' NOTES

From the Photo

Strand and Objectives

Space
- build structures and make geometric models, analysing their cross-sections and nets

Attitudes
- exhibit a willingness to persist when solving problems and to try different methods of attack

Mathematical Inquiry
- test conjectures in space and number and search for counter-examples

Duration 60 minutes
Group size 6 children working in pairs
Materials
60 triangles, 25 squares, 2 pentagons, a blacklead pencil, grid paper, ruler and eraser per pair

1. To achieve success in this activity the children need to:
    - carefully consider what can be seen in the photo
    - consider what Geoshape pieces have been used to construct each model
    - calculate how many of each shape were used in each model
    - perhaps make a 2D net of the 3D model before assembling it

2. For some of the models you may need to give the children a clue as to the exact number and type of Geoshapes required:
    - model 1 consists of 10 triangles
    - model 2 consists of 15 squares, 2 pentagons
    - model 3 consists of 18 squares, 8 triangles
    - model 4 consists of 24 triangles
    - model 5 consists of 60 triangles

3. Vocabulary that you could encourage the children to be using with you and with each other includes: *view, viewpoints, three-dimensional, 3D, nets, models ...*

4. Encourage the children to discuss the clues they find in the photos.

5. The children can self-assess their own models by matching their completed versions with the photos in the activity. They may also present their models and have a brief interview with you on how they went about making them. The report may include aspects such as: problems encountered, methods or strategies employed, level of cooperation with partner and other groups, level of enjoyment and achievement and further challenges.

© 3D GEOSHAPES 1995

From the Photo

Follow-up Ideas

1. Children build their own model, initially limiting themselves to Geoshape squares. They draw a top view and front view of their model and count the number of squares they used to create it. Grid paper can be useful in preparing these drawings. eg:

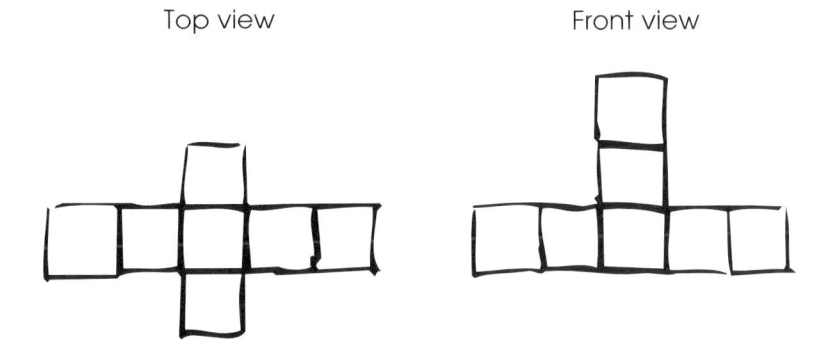

   Top view   Front view

   Models are then dismantled and the children pass their drawings to a partner. The partner, not having seen the model, must then use the top and front drawings, and the clue of the number of squares used, to make a 3D model based on the drawings.

From the Photo

1. 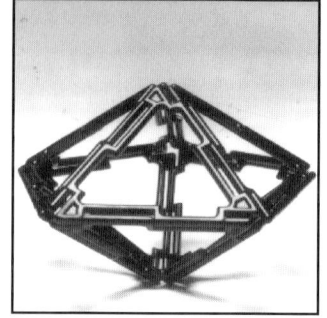
2. 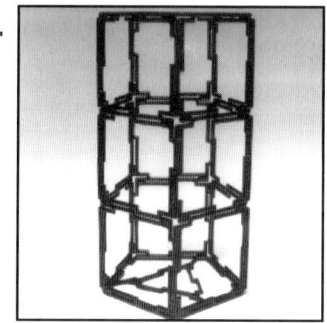
3. 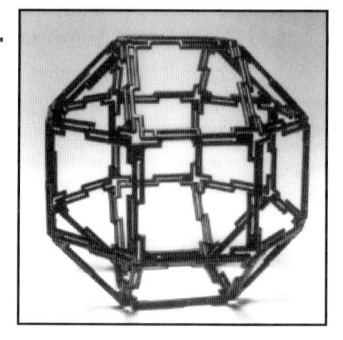
4.

Here are five photos of 3D models made with Geoshape pieces. The challenge for you and a partner is to try and build each model from the photo. They start easy and get harder. Good luck!

5.

For some of the models it may help to first make a net, rather than starting to build it in one go.

What Value?

TEACHERS' NOTES

Strand and Objectives

Attitudes
- demonstrate the confidence to apply mathematics and to gain knowledge about mathematics

Choosing and Using Mathematics
- choose and use mathematical skills to make decisions
- clarify and pose problems arising in practical or imagined contexts

Number
- use whole numbers and decimal fractions to count and order collections and measures
- remember basic addition and multiplication facts and perform mental computations on whole numbers and money

Algebra
- represent (verbally, graphically, in writing and physically) and interpret relationships between quantities

Duration 45 minutes

Group size Pairs

Materials
18 triangles and triangle dot paper per pair

1. In the activity the answer to question 3 is 18, and the answer to question 4 is 54.
2. Giving the shapes different values and using more than one shape can open doors in algebra and fractions. eg:
   - Use a square. Give it the value of one half. Make a shape worth 5, 6, 7, 8 ...
   - This row of houses could be valued as: 6 x (3 + 5) or (6 x 3) + (6 x 5)

   This is a powerful demonstration that: 6 x (3 + 5) = (6 x 3) + (6 x 5)

Follow-up Ideas

1. Ask the children to make a 2D shape using a restricted number of any Geoshapes. In advance prepare number cards which will fit inside the different Geoshapes. Give one card per shape to each child and ask them to calculate the value of their design.
2. Work in reverse by giving children a total value and requiring them to make the equivalent design, firstly using just one type of Geoshape and then using 2 or more. The children will have to decide the values to assign to the Geoshapes to reach the total.
3. Use the same value relations concept to create a 3D object.

© 3D GEOSHAPES 1995

What Value?

If the triangle has the value 1, then this shape has the value of 2.

1. With your partner, use triangles to build a shape worth 3?

2. How many ways can you build a 2D shape with a value of 4, 5, 6, 7?

   Draw each one you make on triangle dot paper.

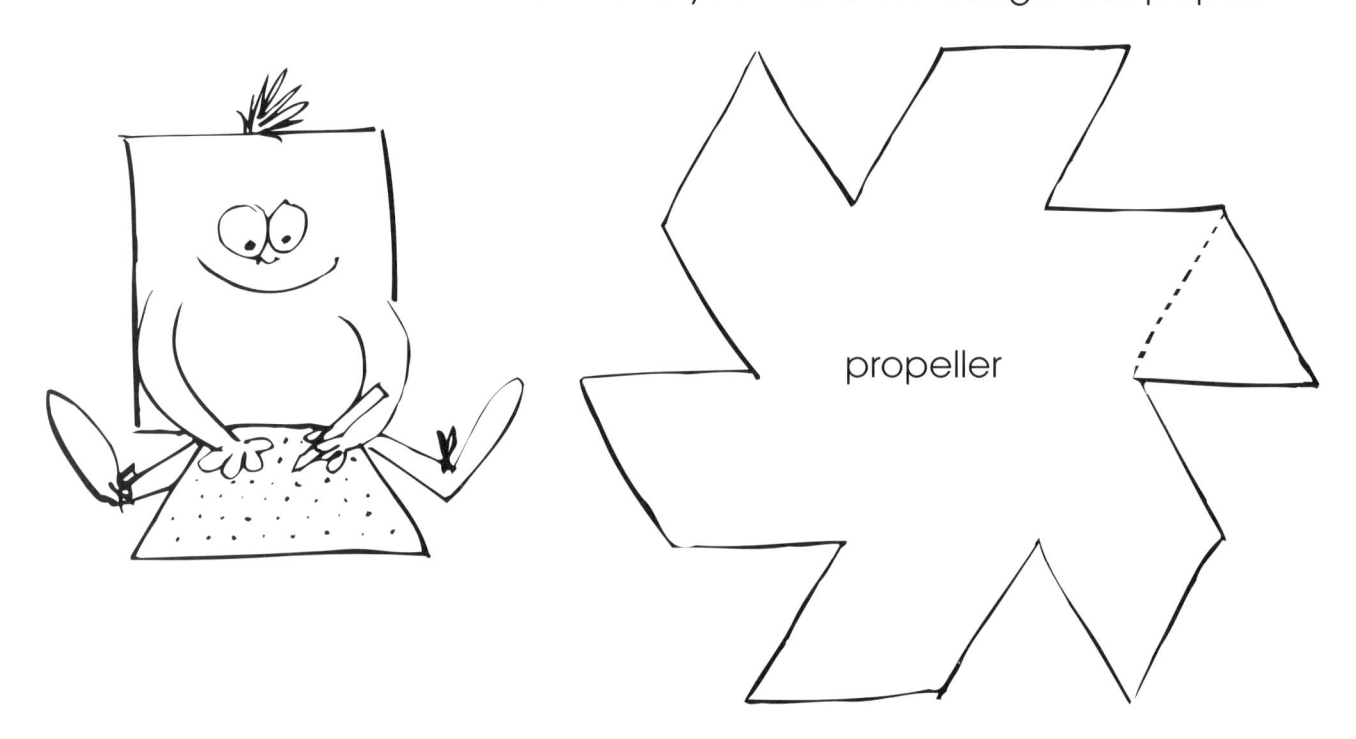

3. Guess the value of the *propeller*.

   Check your guess by making the shape and counting.

4. What would be its value if the triangle was worth 3?

Count the Squares

TEACHERS' NOTES

Strand and Objectives

Attitudes

- exhibit a willingness to persist when solving problems and to try different methods of attack
- understand that mathematics involves observing, generalising and representing patterns

Choosing and Using Mathematics

- clarify and pose problems arising in practical or imagined contexts
- verify and interpret solutions with respect to the original problem

Algebra

- use verbal expressions (oral or written) to describe and summarise spatial or numerical patterns

Mathematical Inquiry

- observe, represent and extend spatial and number patterns

Duration 30 minutes

Group size Pairs

Materials

36 squares per pair

1. In Activity A the total number of squares is 91. However it is the system that the children use to determine and record all the squares which is important.
2. A helpful pattern is to consider each size separately:

    6 x 6 square =   1
    5 x 5 squares =   4
    4 x 4 squares =   9
    3 x 3 squares = 16
    2 x 2 squares = 25
    1 x 1 squares = 36
                          91

3. Some children find it helpful when counting, say, the 3 x 3 squares to make a separate 3 x 3 square and slide it across the 6 x 6 square in an organised way, counting as they go.
4. Another hint useful to some children is realising that if there are four squares across then there must be four down, however, try not to give too many clues too early.

Follow-up Ideas

1. Try Activity A with a flat triangle 6 x 6 x 6. See the activity *How Many Triangles?*

© 3D GEOSHAPES 1995

Count the Squares A

1. With your partner, use 36 squares to make a large flat 6 x 6 square.

   What size squares can you see?

   There are the little 1 x 1 squares and there is the big 6 x 6 square.

   Can you see the 5 x 5 squares? How many are there?

   Count the number of squares altogether in this grid? (Hint: there are more than 80)

2. This table might help you record your work.

Size of Square	How Many?
6x6	1
5x5	
4x4	
3x3	
2x2	
1x1	
Total	

Count the Squares B

1. Guess how many squares there would be altogether if you made a large flat 3 x 3 square. Make the 3 x 3 square and check your guess.

2. Guess again for another large flat square of your choice. Check your guess by making it.

3. Without making the squares can you work out how many squares there would be altogether in a 7 x 7 square, an 8 x 8 square and a 10 x 10 square. You might like to use a calculator to help.

4. Record your results. Can you see any patterns?

Make It Bigger

TEACHERS' NOTES

Strand and Objectives

Space
- compare and classify figures, analyse their shapes and describe in conventional geometric language
- reduce and enlarge figures and objects and investigate distortions resulting from transformations

Chance & Data
- systematically collect, organise and record data to answer questions
- represent, interpret and report on data in order to answer questions

Measurement
- choose appropriate units for tasks by considering purpose, and the need for precision and/or communication

Number
- recognise, produce and use patterns in number

Mathematical Inquiry
- observe, represent and extend spatial and number patterns

Duration   45 minutes
Group size   Pairs
Materials
At least 16 triangles and 16 squares per pair

1. This activity has many aspects:
   - the introduction of the concepts of perimeter and area
   - the recognition that both concepts are only measurable in terms of a chosen unit
   - the recognition that to compare perimeter and area of different shapes the unit used to measure must be the same.
   - recording data in an organised manner to assist with the recognition of patterns

2. Activity A leads into these aspects from within the safe environment of squares. However, children may need to be shown how to use the Geoshape square to measure perimeter and area.
   eg: The perimeter of the square below is 8 edges of a Geoshape square and its area is 4 Geoshape squares.

Make It Bigger

3. Organising data and looking for patterns may reveal results such as this one for squares:

Length of one side of square	Perimeter of square	Area of square
1	4	1
2	8	4
3	12	9

4. Activity B allows the children more choice and consequently is more open ended. If the children *choose* to increase the linear dimensions proportionally (double, triple, quadruple ...) they will be led to the same relationships as in Activity A. Doubling linear measurements increases area measurements four fold, regardless of the unit chosen to count the perimeter and area. Similarly, tripling the linear dimensions leads to an area 9 times larger and so on.

    However, if the children *choose* to change their shape by adding or subtracting a number of units, they will be led to a more general relationship of which the proportional case is a specific example.

5. Encourage children to make predictions based on the patterns they discover.

Follow-up Ideas

1. Challenge children to check their discoveries for shapes made from a mixture of triangles and squares. The triangle and square pieces are the same length along an edge, so perimeter is relatively straight forward to count in each case. However counting area introduces the need to decide on only one measurement unit and the need to estimate for some shapes. The triangle is not half the area of a square, but that is the most likely approximation that the children will use. It is a reasonable one, but they should be challenged to explain their reasoning. Some possible challenges are:
    - Join a triangle to a square. Try making that shape bigger.
    - Join a triangle to each side of a rectangle. Try to enlarge that shape.
2. Try making other shapes such as a pentagon or an octagon.
3. Try making a recognisable shape which uses triangles, squares and pentagons.

Make It Bigger A

* For this activity use only squares. One Geoshape square is your measurement unit. *

1. Make a square of any size.
2. Use your measurement *unit* to:
   - count the number of edges which fit around the outside of the square you made. This number is called the *perimeter* of your square.
   - count the number of units it would take to cover your square. This number is called the *area* of your square.
3. Record the perimeter and area of your square.
4. Now make a different size square. Count and record the perimeter and area this time.
5. Continue making different size squares. Count and record the perimeter and area each time.
6. Organise your results and look for patterns. Write a report about what you find.

Make It Bigger B

* For this activity, use squares *or* triangles, but not both at once.*

1. Make one of these shapes.

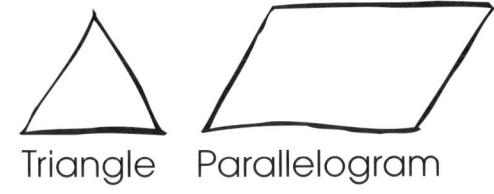

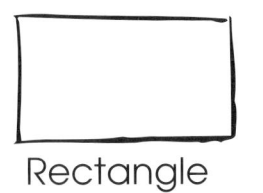

   Triangle   Parallelogram   Rectangle   Hexagon

2. Count and record the perimeter and area of the shape. Choose the best shape to use as your measurement *unit*.

3. Now make the shape again in a different size. Count and record the perimeter and area this time.

4. Continue making the shape in different sizes. Count and record the perimeter and area each time.

5. Repeat the activity with the other shapes.

6. Organise your results and look for patterns. Write a report about what you find.

TEACHERS' NOTES

How Many Triangles?

Strand and Objectives

Attitudes
- understand that mathematics involves observing, generalising and representing patterns
- appreciate that the economy and power of mathematical notation and terminology help in developing mathematical ideas

Algebra
- use verbal expressions (oral or written) to describe and summarise spatial or numerical patterns
- make and use arithmetic generalisations

Mathematical Inquiry
- observe, represent and extend spatial and number patterns

Duration   30 - 45 minutes
Group Size   Pairs
Materials
16 triangles per pair

1. For the triangle shown in the activity, the counting is:
   16 Size 1 triangles, 9 Size 2 triangles, 4 Size 3 triangles and 1 Size 4 triangle.
   Which gives a total of 30 triangles of various sizes.
2. The totals for triangles Size 1, Size 2 and Size 3 can be found in a similar way. The totals are:
   Size 1 = 1   just the Geoshape piece itself
   Size 2 = 5   1 x Size 2 + 4 x Size 1
   Size 3 = 14   1 x Size 3 + 4 x Size 2 + 9 x Size 1
3. Similarly the Size 6 triangle would give a total of $1 + 4 + 9 + 16 + 25 + 36 = 91$
4. In the general case:
   Total triangles of all sizes in a Size n triangle = $1 + 4 + 9 + ... (n-1)^2 + n^2$
5. The children might notice that this result is the same as the result in the activity *Count the Squares*.

Follow-up Ideas

1. Compare the results obtained in this activity with those in *Count the Squares*. Can the children suggest why the same pattern appears.
2. It is instructive to graph the Size of the triangle against the number of Size 1 triangles which can be counted inside it. The points lie on a parabola, but they cannot sensibly be joined up. Why? This is probably the children's first experience with a set of pairs which don't produce a straight line.

© 3D GEOSHAPES 1995

How Many Triangles?

1. Make this Size 4 triangle:

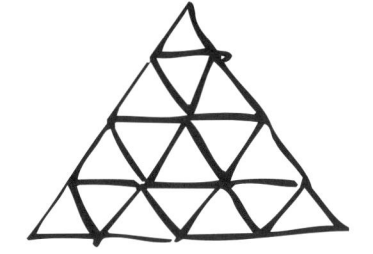

2. How many triangles of any size can you count? There are 16 Size 1 triangles and 1 Size 4 triangle, but how many altogether? Organise your counting so that you can be sure you have them all.

3. Make the Size 1, Size 2 and Size 3 triangles in turn. Each time predict and then check the total number of triangles.

4. Predict the number of triangles altogether in the Size 6 triangle. You could check by drawing on triangle dot paper.

5. Can you work out a rule for counting the total number of triangles in a Size n triangle?

Adapted from the Mathematics Task Centre Project and used with permission of Curriculum Corporation.

TEACHERS' NOTES

Pointy Fences

Strand and Objectives

Space

- build structures and make geometric models, analysing their cross-sections and nets

Choosing and Using Mathematics

- choose and use mathematical skills to make decisions
- clarify and pose problems arising in practical or imagined contexts

Mathematical Inquiry

- draw diagrams and read and write mathematics using simple formulae, pictures, tables and statistical graphs
- observe, represent and extend spatial and number patterns

Duration 30 - 45 minutes

Group size Pairs

Materials

8 triangles and 10 squares per pair

1. A Number 1 fence needs 4 triangles and 8 squares = 12 pieces.
   A Number 2 fence needs 8 triangles and 10 squares = 18 pieces.
   A Number 3 fence needs 12 triangles and 12 squares = 24 pieces.
2. A Number 100 fence needs 400 triangles and 206 squares = 606 pieces. Since a Number 100 fence has 100 points and each point requires 4 triangles, it needs 400 triangles. Each point has a square on either side of it, and requires 3 extra squares at each end, which gives the total of 206 squares.
3. It is important to first ask the children to explain their working out and then to write their explanation. Their explanation may vary from the description above.

Follow-up Ideas

1. Demonstrate how formulas can be entered in a spreadsheet to reflect the patterns discovered, and then how the spreadsheet has the power to build on the entries in the first row to find answers for any size fence. The table shows the *formulas* which are entered and then copied down.

	A	B	C	D
1	Fence Number	Triangles	Square	Total
2	1	=4* A2	=2* A2 + 6	=B2 + C2
3	=A2 + 1			

© 3D GEOSHAPES 1995

Pointy Fences

1. The Fabulous Fencing Company makes fences like this in any length:

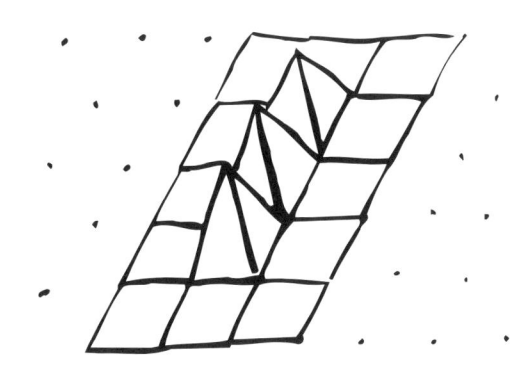

    This is a Number 3 fence. Each face of the pyramids is made with one triangle. They are then surrounded by one width of squares as shown in the picture.

2. Make a Number 1 and a Number 2 fence. How many Geoshape pieces are used to make each one?

3. Work out from the picture above, the number of pieces needed to make a Number 3 fence?

4. Try to draw the next few sizes of fence. Work out the number of Geoshapes needed for each one.

5. Imagine the Number 100 fence. Work out the number of pieces needed to make it. Explain your answer.

Adapted from the Mathematics Task Centre Project and used with permission of Curriculum Corporation.

Tetrahedron Triangles

TEACHERS' NOTES

Strand and Objectives

Space
- build structures and make geometric models, analysing their cross-sections and nets
- plan and execute arrangements according to specifications

Attitudes
- understand that mathematics involves observing, generalising and representing patterns

Number
- recognise, produce and use patterns in number

Mathematical Inquiry
- observe, represent and extend spatial and number patterns

Duration 30 minutes

Group size Pairs

Materials
16 triangles and triangle dot paper per pair

1. The completed table for question 4 in the activity is:

Tetrahedron Size	1	2	3	4	5	10	100
Total number of triangles to make the tetrahedron	4	16	36	64	100	400	40,000

2. The number of triangle pieces in each face is the square of the number of triangles along one edge. So to find the total number of triangles for any size tetrahedron, square the Size number (which is the same as the number of triangles along one edge) and, because there are four faces, multiply by 4.

3. Encourage the children to verbalise and record this rule. Explore how to record it in shorthand. When algebra grows from a context, children can attach meaning to the terms. So, in this case, it is not difficult for them to comprehend that this experiment is summarised by the rule: $T = 4 \times S^2$, where T is the number of Triangles and S is the Size of the tetrahedron.

Follow-up Ideas

1. Graph the number pairs in the table up to a Size 5 tetrahedron. Teach the children how to freehand draw the curve which links them and extend it (extrapolate is the mathematical word) to predict the total for the Sizes 6, 7, 8, 9, 10 tetrahedrons. Check against the pattern they have discovered. Explore whether the curve gives any acceptable information where it has been drawn between the plotted points.

© 3D GEOSHAPES 1995

Tetrahedron Triangles

1. Make this Size 1 tetrahedron:

   It is called Size 1 because each edge is one unit long.

2. Make one face of a Size 2 tetrahedron like this:

   The edge of each face is two units long. Now put four faces together to make a Size 2 tetrahedron.

3. Make one face of a Size 3 tetrahedron. Record it on the triangle dot paper.

4. Use what you have made so far and the dot paper to help you fill in this table:

Tetrahedron Size	1	2	3	4	5	10	100
Total number of triangles to make the tetrahedron	4	16					

5. Explain how to work out the number of triangles for a tetrahedron of *any* size.

Adapted from the Mathematics Task Centre Project and used with permission of Curriculum Corporation.

THEME IDEAS

The Beach

1. Create a beach scene on a table with blue crepe paper for the ocean and yellow crepe paper for the sand. Use your Geoshapes to make:
   - banana lounges
   - a life saver's lookout tower
   - beach umbrellas
   - beach balls
   - a pier from the sand to the water
   - a kiosk
   - bathing boxes
   - ships, yachts, canoes, surf boards

2. Above your scene suspend:
   - the sun
   - a shark spotting plane
   - a news helicopter
   - seagulls
   - hang-gliders, paragliders

   Use other art materials to enhance your scene.

2. Design and make your own perfect beach chair. It might have a built in drink cooler, umbrella, cushions, footrests and adjustable positions.

3. Design and build an interesting beach-mobile that can be used in the sea and on the sand. It may have fold down sails that catch the wind and big spherical wheels.

Dinosaurs

THEME IDEAS

1. Create a prehistoric scene using various art materials. Use your Geoshapes to make the dinosaurs you would expect to find living in this environment, such as:
   - stegosaurus with plates on its back and spikes on its tail
   - triceratops with a frill-like collar and horns on its head
   - ankylosaurus with its armour of spikes
   - the huge tyrannosaurus rex
   - baby dinosaurs hatching from eggs
   - reptiles with wings

2. Make your own imaginary prehistoric monster using Geoshapes. Give your monster a name and write a story about the world it lived in.

3. Pretend your are a dinosaur. Use Geoshapes to make something you can wear so other children will know which dinosaur you are. eg:
   - spiky backbones, capes or tails
   - masks with big pointed teeth and horns
   - sails that attach to your back
   - collar frills

© 3D GEOSHAPES 1995

THEME IDEAS

Our Community

1. Lay masking tape out around the carpet to create a system of roads and blocks.
2. Design buildings and facilities for the community such as:
   - shops
   - schools
   - houses
   - parks
   - playground equipment
3. Design a sports centre. It might have:
   - tennis courts
   - basketball courts
   - viewing area
   - swimming pools
   - cafeteria
4. Make some sports equipment:
   - ball and bat
   - helmet
   - hockey stick
5. As a class, create a model playground using Geoshapes. You could create:
   - monkey bars
   - slides
   - see-saws
   - spaceship rides
   - climbing frames and towers
   - cubby houses
   - cricket stumps
   - a basketball ring and backboard on a pole

Combine the Geoshapes with other art materials.

Our Community

THEME IDEAS

6. Use only triangles and squares to build a ferris wheel or roundabout for a playground.
7. Make a quiet area with bench seats, tables, trees and a bridge.
8. Design an interesting playground 'thing' and describe how to use it.
9. Build a flat aerial view of your ideal playground.

© 3D GEOSHAPES 1995

THEME IDEAS: Space

1. Create a space scene that you can suspend from the ceiling. Use your Geoshapes to build:
    - a space station and space laboratory
    - spacecraft such as Voyager 2 with its dome shaped satellite dish and large aerial
    - space telescopes such as the Hubble telescope with its cylindrical body and rectangular wings
    - space shuttles
    - rockets
2. Create a base station on earth.
    - buildings
    - radio telescopes
    - a rocket or space shuttle launching pad
3. Create a moon scene out of paper mache and rocks. Use your Geoshapes to make:
    - the spacecraft that has just landed
    - moon buggies
    - moon creatures

© 3D GEOSHAPES 1995

Space

THEME IDEAS

4. Create a galaxy of stars and planets using Geoshapes. Suspend your stellated and spherical structures from the ceiling.
5. Design and make a space helmet to fit over your head. It must have an opening flap for access to your face
6. Make a Darth Vader mask.
7. Design and make a life support system to wear on your back. Include an oxygen supply and radio.
8. Build a rocket using only squares and triangles. Add cellophane paper to create a blast-off effect.
9. Build a UFO which can spin, and has a door to let the aliens out. Make an alien.

THEME IDEAS

Transport

1. Make a railway system:
   - tracks
   - boom gates
   - tunnels
   - a station with a raised platform

   Combine your Geoshapes with other materials if you wish.

2. Around your railway system add:
   - trucks, cars, buses
   - a car towing a caravan
   - a semi-trailer
   - a bridge with two lanes to cross the railway line
   - your own 'crazy car'

3. Use only squares and triangles to make a seven carriage train. Is it a passenger train or a freight train? Join the carriages with pipe cleaners.

4. Design a freeway system in the sandpit. Use Geoshapes and other materials to make the signs, bridges, and vehicles.

© 3D GEOSHAPES 1995

Transport

THEME IDEAS

5. Make a car carrying truck which can carry at least two cars. Make the cars that fit it.
6. Make a bridge as long as your table which stands up by itself. It must be able to support the weight of the toy cars which drive over it.
7. Design a special car seat with features that will prevent injury in crashes.
8. Make a helicopter to report traffic conditions. It must have two exits and the rotor must spin. Pop-sticks and toothpicks might help.
9. Use Geoshapes to create the frame of a boat. Cover the frame with something so the boat floats. Race your boats using a fan to create a breeze.
10. Combine Geoshapes with other materials to make a hot air balloon which can support a doll.

Square Grid

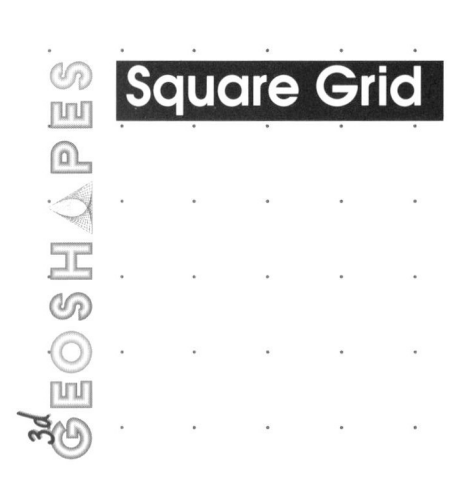

Triangle Grid

Isometric Grid

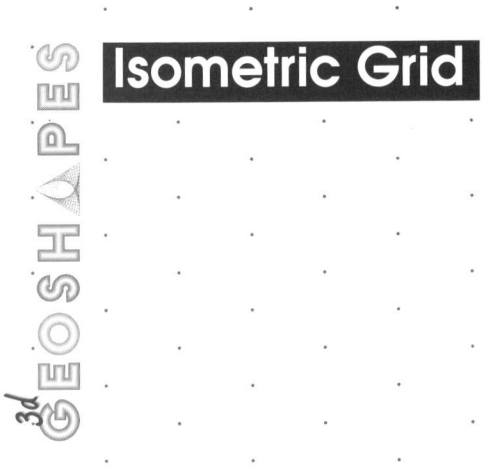